GREAT SOUTHERN MANSIONS

JOZEFA STUART AND WILSON RANDOLPH GATHINGS
WITH AN INTRODUCTION BY ROBERT KORNFELD

A WALKER GALLERY BOOK

WALKER AND COMPANY · 720 FIFTH AVENUE · NEW YORK, NEW YORK 10019

CONTENTS

Introduction *3*

VIRGINIA—Where It All Began *5*

NORTH CAROLINA—Home of the Independent Spirit *16*

SOUTH CAROLINA—Gardens Equal Houses in Grandeur *20*

GEORGIA—Colony with a High Purpose *28*

TENNESSEE—White Pillars in the Land of Plenty *33*

ALABAMA—Lacy Ironwork and Colonnades Abound *40*

MISSISSIPPI—Mansions, Magnolias, Mockingbirds *50*

TEXAS—Land of Cowboys and Cavaliers *58*

LOUISIANA—Grand Parade of Plantation Splendor *62*

A Traveler's Guide *70*

Acknowledgments *72*

STAFF

EDITORIAL DIRECTOR: Richard K. Winslow

ART DIRECTOR: Barbara Huntley

MANAGING EDITOR: Andrea H. Curley

TEXT EDITOR: Virginia Burke

RESEARCH: Judith Szarka

PRODUCTION: David Kellogg

FRONT COVER: D'Evereux, Natchez, Mississippi. A Greek Revival masterpiece built c.1840 by William St. John Elliot.
Photograph by D. Hallinan-FPG.

BACK COVER: Milford Plantation, near Pinewood, South Carolina. Built 1839 by Governor John L. Manning. *See pages 26-27.*
From, Historic American Buildings Survey; photograph by Jack E. Boucher.

OVERLEAF: Monticello, Charlottesville, Virginia. A painting done in 1827 by an unknown artist. *See pages 14-15.*
From, Thomas Jefferson Memorial Foundation; photograph by Ed Roseberry.

ABOVE: Belmont, Nashville, Tennessee. *See pages 34-35, 46.*
From Historic American Buildings Survey; Jack E. Boucher.

OPPOSITE: Shadows-on-the-Teche, New Iberia, Louisiana. *See pages 68-69.*
From The National Trust for Historic Preservation.

All rights reserved under the International Copyright Union by Walker Publishing Company, Inc. No part of this book may be reproduced or transmitted in any form or by any means, electric or mechanical, including photocopying, recording, or by any information storage and retrieval system, without permission in writing from the Publisher.

First published in the United States of America in 1977 by the Walker Publishing Company, Inc.

Published simultaneously in Canada by Beaverbooks, Limited, Pickering, Ontario

Cloth   ISBN: 0-8027-0576-6
Paper   ISBN: 0-8027-7115-7

Library of Congress Catalog Card Number: 77-78129

Printed in Japan by Dai Nippon Printing Co., Ltd., Tokyo

10 9 8 7 6 5 4 3 2 1

Introduction

MORE THAN A century ago, sometime back in the 1840s, a young woman named Eliza Ripley stepped off a Mississippi River packet boat onto the landing of one of the South's great plantations. In her memoirs, written many years later when she was in her nineties, she recalled the occasion. The trip from New Orleans had been wonderfully strange and exciting for her, the passenger cabin friendly as a tea party, and the little river boat pausing now and then along the way to drop off packets of mail and crates of fresh fruit. Now she had arrived at her destination, the plantation of Valcour Aime. It was evening, and through the darkness she beheld in awe the flames of torches carried by a long procession of servants who had been sent to meet her party. A fellow guest was carried to the house on a flat car along tracks laid especially for the occasion, borrowed from the plantation's private railway built to carry cane in from the fields. The night was cool, and Eliza was delighted to find the fireplace in her room ablaze. She was promptly treated to a traditional Creole footbath and a steaming herb tisane to sip before she fell off to sleep.

The next morning, Eliza was welcomed for breakfast by the entire family. The dining room, she remembered, was large and open to the outdoors, "redolent of the delicious odor of roses." After breakfast, she was shown through a "seemingly endless series of living and sleeping rooms" and an equally endless number of gardens and groves. That day and the days following, she was treated to a round of parties and visits to the neighboring plantations. More than sixty years later, Eliza ended her memoir by saying she did not care to know what had happened to the Aime family, afraid of discovering after so long a time what she had discovered about others. "I already know of too many wrecked homes and vanished fortunes and broken hearts," she wrote. "I want always to think of the Valcour Aime home and its charming hospitality as I saw it, and loved it . . . when I waved a last adieu—alas! a last."

Neither pictures nor words can duplicate Eliza's real-life experience, but this book can serve as a literary vehicle carrying the reader up rivers, as Eliza's packet boat had carried her, and across roads inland, as horse-and-carriage had carried travelers in past centuries, to the great plantation homes of a pre-Civil War South. The reader can view with wonder for the first time, as Eliza did, the white-pillared porticos, the breezy galleries and graceful balconies, the sweeping verandas and grand ballrooms, the formal gardens and paths lined with pine, oak, mimosa and magnolia, all of which characterize the antebellum plantation of the old South. The book is intended as a sampler rather than a complete guide, for armchair architects and for all who find pleasure and value in exploring an exotic part of the American past. This past, in its way, continues to flower through the presence of these great houses, which evoke their own aura of a faraway life and time. The photographs—32 pages of color and 32 pages of black-and-white—record the existence today of many of the South's finest plantation and town houses, throughout Virginia, the Carolinas, Georgia, Tennessee, Alabama, Louisiana, Mississippi, and Texas.

Romantic myths and true stories relate the richness, in both human and material terms, of America's plantation homes. "We shall be the richest people beneath the bend of the rainbow," wrote an enthusiastic Georgian in 1840, and Southern planters were indeed the wealthiest men in America. Over a two-hundred-year period they built for themselves the most magnificent of all American private houses—the Southern mansion. Hundreds of these superb structures stand today, and among them are enduring examples of a distinctive yet diverse architecture, covering roughly the two centuries before the Civil War. The "sightseer" on this journey may view, in one reading, Jacobean, Georgian, Federal, Greek Revival, Gothic, and Victorian.

In his travels, the visitor to old plantation houses may feel the presence of abiding ghosts—for example, that of a lovely young woman living at Parlange Plantation in Louisiana, whose domineering mother forced her to marry a man not of her choice and soon died of a broken heart; and that of the lady of Arlington in Natchez who, on the morning after a lavish house-warming given to celebrate her moving in, was found dead in bed under mysterious circumstances.

Plantation houses are also haunted by the ghosts of great men. George Washington and Thomas Jefferson were masters of plantations, and both were superior agriculturists of their times. Washington considerably increased the acreage and productivity of Mount Vernon, practicing crop rotation and contour ploughing a century and a half before twentieth century agronomists "discovered" such techniques. Thomas Jefferson acquired seeds from all corners of the world, experimented endlessly with plants, and invented a much-improved version of the moldboard plough, a major technical advance in farming methods and one of his great prides. His legacy to today's traveler is Monticello, the classically beautiful hilltop home in Virginia which he designed and built for his family.

James Madison and James Monroe, two other Virginians who became President, also owned great houses. And Andrew Jackson, seventh President of the United States, became a successful cotton planter and owned a great house, although he was better known as a rough backwoods man-of-the-people. His last home, The Hermitage, near Nashville, stands today as one of the South's finest Greek Revival plantation houses—an idealization of the classicism of an ancient age.

Today, men of fabulous wealth are referred to as tycoons, oil barons, financiers, business entrepeneurs, and industrialists. But from 1660 to 1860, when agriculture was the main "business" of the United States, the "Southern planter" reigned supreme. One of this land aristocracy was Valcour Aime (Eliza Ripley's host), owner of vast acres of sugar cane plantations along the Mississippi above New Orleans. He was, in his time, the richest man in the South, sneering at bankers and paying hard cash for farmlands, riverboats, and houses and gardens said to rival those at Versailles. He filled the cages of his private zoo with animals from all over the world. When Valcour Aime's only son died, he ordered a new church built in a neighboring town, and then sank into a hopeless depression from which he suffered the rest of his life. His house and gardens fell into ruin as he wandered about the plantation, always in black, and thus became one of the area's most exotic legendary figures. And to add a final fillip to this strange and tragic tale, the Mississippi River changed its course and swallowed up the new church soon after it was completed.

Generosity and hospitality seem to grow naturally when wealth is prodigious, and so Southern generosity and hospitality reached high peaks during this period. Generosity was exhibited by Thomas, Lord Fairfax, a cousin of George Washington's sister-in-law. Young George, a surveyor by trade when still in his teens, earned enough money surveying the Fairfax five-and-a-half-million acres (which included the entire Shenandoah Valley) to start investing in land before he was twenty. And Lord Fairfax, wondering whatever to do with his millions of unsettled acres, gave away hundreds to a number of churches, and once even tipped a man with a piece of property for holding his horse. Following his liberal tendencies, Fairfax allowed his agent, Robert Carter, to accumulate some 330,000 acres in Virginia. With such holdings, Mr. Carter became one of the most powerful figures in the state and is still spoken of with awe as "King Carter."

A century later, generosity continued to proliferate at princely levels. William Harding, of Belle Meade Plantation, near Nashville, gave $5 million to the Southern cause at the time of the Civil War. And in Louisiana, Valcour Aime slipped $3,000 under the dinner plates of his children each Christmas, and gave them all plantations as wedding presents.

Southern hospitality, no myth, reached full flower during the great mansion era. These were days without railroads or paved highways, when travel was slow and country inns were few and far apart, and hotels were found only in major cities. Consequently, dinner guests coming from more than a few miles away had to stay overnight. Thomas Jefferson often fed and housed as many as fifty at a time. In fact, his lavish hospitality—he entertained dozens of overnight guests with fine French wines and exquisite poultry and meats—reduced the former President to near poverty in his later years.

Valcour Aime kept a spare room always prepared for strangers; it was known up and down the Mississippi that anyone who asked would be provided the room, plus dinner and breakfast. And a visitor's clothes would always be brushed and pressed while he slept. Throughout Mississippi, plantation houses were often built with a "stranger's room" in the main house for unexpected—and unknown—overnight guests, a room that opened, however, onto the outer gallery instead of the home's inner hallway.

When the plantation and its accompanying way of life began to appear in America in the 1600s, sugar cane fields did not exist in Louisiana, nor did rice fields in Georgia. America's first plantation sprouted in the state of Virginia, and John Rolfe was its master.

The first Virginia settlers had been brought over by Sir Walter Raleigh during the reign of Queen Elizabeth I, and agriculture was introduced thirty-five years later near the first permanent English settlement in America, Jamestown, founded in 1607 and named for Elizabeth's successor, King James I. Although John Rolfe may be better remembered romantically as John Smith's successful rival for the hand of Pocahontas, he played a more significant role in history by growing America's first agricultural crop to be shipped back to and sold in England. The year was 1620, and the crop was tobacco.

Thus began a plantation way of life which spread steadily throughout the South for the next 240 years. Stories of prosperity in Virginia soon attracted the more adventurous and ambitious men from England. John Washington (George's great-grandfather), born in England in 1632, sailed off to the new American colony, and in 1665 set up a mill on the banks of Rozier's Creek in King George County. He prospered, and in 1669 applied for a grant to certain farmland, the first parcel of what was eventually to become the Mount Vernon estate, eighty-six years before his great-grandson became master of Mount Vernon in 1775. By American Revolution time in 1776, a century of plantation life had already been enjoyed in Virginia. Grand white-pillared houses had been built by newly rich planters on their increasingly vast private lands.

The Carolinas were next to develop an agrarian wealth. Further south but still along the coast, Carolina growers had easy access to ships which carried their crops across the sea to England. It was well after 1700 before pioneers from the seacoasts of Virginia and the Carolinas began moving in to the highlands some twenty or thirty miles from the shore. The first permanent settlement of Englishmen in Tennessee was
Continued on page 69

Virginia—Where It All Began

ENGLISH SETTLEMENT of the American colonies began in Virginia—at Jamestown, in 1607—as did the plantation system of agriculture. Named after Elizabeth I, the Virgin Queen, the state is called the Old Dominion because it remained loyal to the Stuart kings during the English Civil Wars of 1642-49. The cavalier tradition has always been strong in Virginia. Long before several other Southern states had established settlements, Virginia had a thriving, aristocratic plantation society. It was the largest in size and population of the colonies. Later, as a state, it gave the Republic four of its first five Presidents. Though some of Virginia's mansions are gone, many still stand, delighting the eye and stirring the imagination. Together, these houses epitomize a vanished world, based on hereditary privilege and landed wealth, whose hallmarks were lavish hospitality and an exquisite refinement of taste. On the following pages are eight of Virginia's grand houses. In some ways they are architecturally similar, but each bears a distinct mark that sets it apart and makes it unforgettable.

CHATHAM, near Falmouth, Virginia. Great houses are often the result of great family alliances. Such is the case with Chatham (*above*). It was built about 1770 after the marriage of William Fitzhugh and Anne Randolph of Chatsworth. Only one room deep, the house with its dependencies is one of the longest in America, and is also notable for its large scale. The site is exceptionally fine—broad terraces fall away from the south front and cut into the high banks of the Rappahannock River. Magnificent plantings of mature boxwood enhance the grounds. During the Civil War, President Lincoln visited the plantation while the Union Army occupied the house. Nearby, within the sound of gunshot, Fitzhughs and Randolphs were fighting and dying for the way of life that Chatham symbolizes. The cause was lost, but its monuments live on—timeless in their beauty, commanding in their dignity, haunting in their presence.

ABOVE: Courtesy, Historical American Buildings Survey, photograph by Jack E. Boucher

BACON'S CASTLE, Surry County, Virginia. A unique survivor of the middle 1600s, this High-Jacobean house (*opposite, top*) proves that there was no Renaissance architectural influence in Virginia at the time. It is in a fine state of preservation and is distinguished by its curvilinear gables and triple-stack chimneys. Standing on the flat fields of southeastern Virginia, surrounded by hollies and great magnolias, Bacon's Castle is an incomparable vision of 17th-century America.

STRATFORD HALL, near Montrose, Virginia. Built about 1725 by Thomas Lee, first native-born Virginian to be governor of the colony, Stratford (*opposite, below*) was the seat of four generations of Lees, ending with Robert E. Lee, symbol of all that was truly great about the Old South. The house is the oldest of Virginia's 18th-century brick mansions and the most monumental in design. There is no house like it in all America. The chimneys and grand exterior stairs of this huge H-shaped house have no counterpart. The Birth Chamber (*below*) was refinished around 1800. Here General Lee was born. His net-drapped cradle rests in a corner of the room. Stratford was restored by the Robert E. Lee Memorial Association and is open to the public. The plantation still grows corn, hay, and barley. In the large detached kitchen, a fire crackles during the winter months, and cider and homemade ginger cookies await hungry visitors.

BELOW AND OPPOSITE BELOW: Courtesy, Robert E. Lee Memorial Association
OPPOSITE ABOVE: Courtesy, Historic American Buildings Survey, photograph by Jack E. Boucher

"One of the Most Elegant Habitations in Virginia"

CARTER'S GROVE, near Williamsburg, Virginia. The oldest of the great mansions are those along the James River. Of these, Carter's Grove (*above*) embodies the most perfect blend of design, detail, and location. Standing on land that the rich and powerful Robert "King" Carter once owned, it was built by his grandson Carter Burwell about 1750. No expense was spared—a master woodworker was brought specially from England, and the house was six years in the building. In 1778, a French visitor, Madame Hélène-Louise de Chastenay Maussion, recorded in her diary: " . . . we stopped at a famous place called Carter Grove, near James River, one of the most elegant habitations in Virginia." The entrance salon (*opposite, bottom*) is considered the finest paneled room in Virginia. The wood is yellow pine. The parlor (*opposite, top*) is known as the Refusal Room because, according to legend, both Washington and Jefferson offered proposals, during social gatherings here, to young ladies and were turned down. Carter's Grove is owned by Colonial Williamsburg and exhibited to show how Virginia planters of the period lived, in contrast to the gentry in town.

ALL PHOTOGRAPHS: Courtesy, The Colonial Williamsburg Foundation

MOUNT AIRY, near Warsaw, Virginia. Considered by many the finest Palladian mansion built in the British colonies, it is unquestionably the finest American house in that style (*below*). Construction was begun in 1758 by John Tayloe on his ancestral acres. The north front, shown here, was inspired by the Italianate Haddo House in Scotland. Unlike most houses of the period, Mount Airy still has its original connections, dependencies, and flanking outbuildings. Its site on the ridge overlooking the Rappahannock River Valley, and its meticulously graded landscape setting, heighten its magnificent architectural effect.

KENMORE, Fredericksburg, Virginia. Colonel Fielding Lewis brought his bride, Betty Washington (George's sister), to this superb Georgian house in 1752. Shown here (*opposite, right*) is the library, with card table set up, ready for the game to begin. All the rooms are perfectly appointed. Of special interest are many objects that belonged to the Washington, Ball, and Lewis families. Kenmore is justly famous for its fine decorative plasterwork—ceilings and overmantels.

LEFT: Courtesy, Historic American Buildings Survey, photograph by Jack E. Boucher
ABOVE: Courtesy, Kenmore Association, photograph by Louis H. Frohman

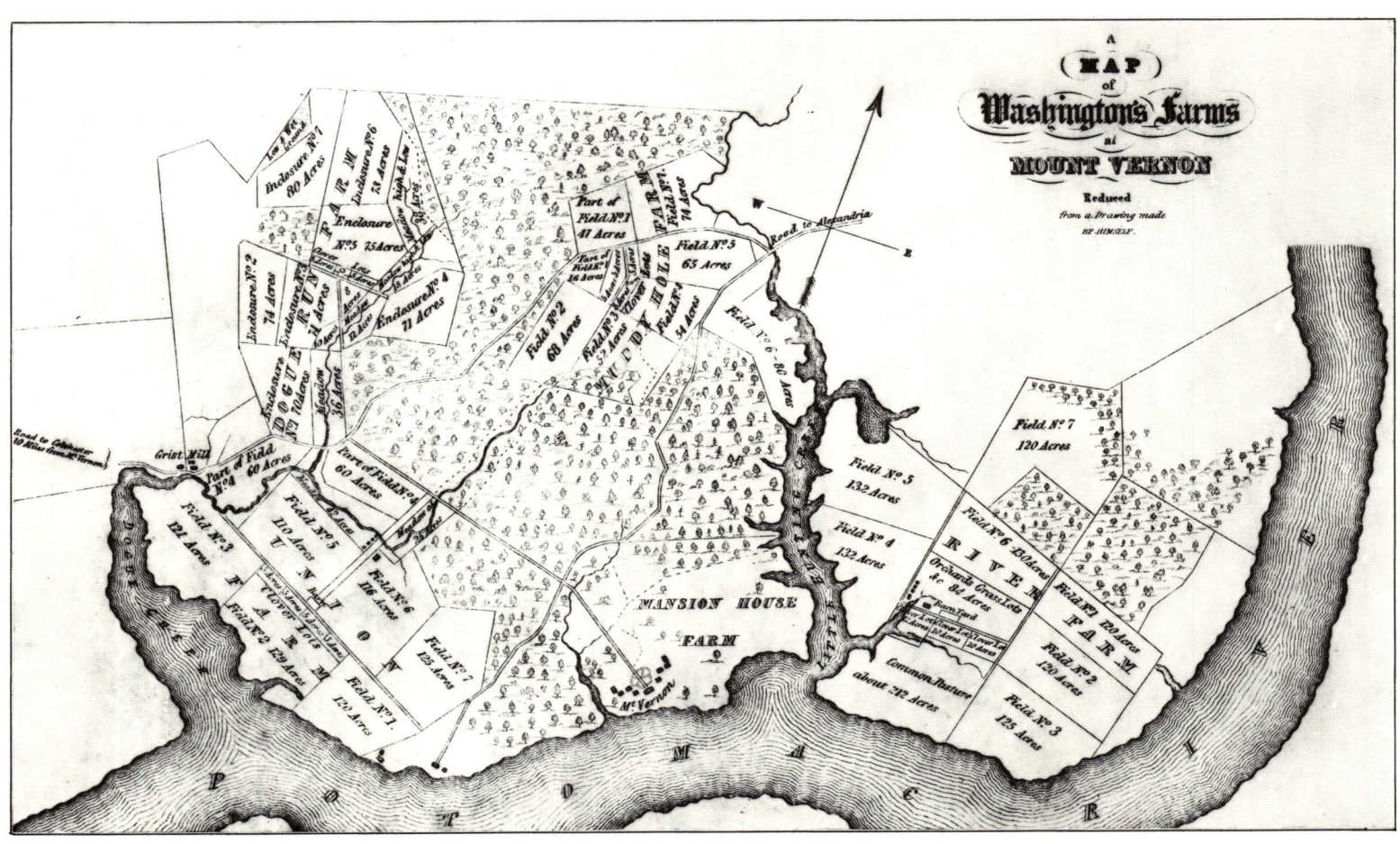

Mansions of Presidents

MOUNT VERNON, near Alexandria, Virginia. George Washington's military genius is known to all, but he was equally brilliant as a surveyor and cartographer. This is evident in the map drawn by him of his farms in 1785 (*above*). Washington was one of the first planters to practice rotation of crops, realizing that the constant cultivation of tobacco exhausted the land. An early painting of the west front, land side, of Mount Vernon (*opposite, top*) depicts members of the family frolicking on the lawn. Washington inherited the house in 1754, one and a half stories at the time, from his half-brother, Lawrence. Afterward, George altered the house, making it two stories and lengthening it from five to nine bays. The view of the east front (*opposite, bottom*) reveals its dramatic perch high above the Potomac River. Washington added the portico in 1784. The architectural precedent for it is unknown, and it is unique of its period.

ABOVE: From *The Life of George Washington* by Jared Sparks, 1844
ABOVE RIGHT: Courtesy, National Gallery of Art
BELOW RIGHT: Courtesy, National Gallery of Art

MONTICELLO, Charlottesville, Virginia. There exists in history no closer relationship between a man and a house than that of Jefferson and Monticello, "little mountain." For over forty years, its construction was the Founding Father's major avocation: "Architecture is my delight, and putting up and pulling down, one of my favorite amusements." Mr. Jefferson's bedroom (*opposite, bottom*) was also his study. The placement of the bed in a passage between two rooms provided ventilation. "All my wishes end where I hope my days will end, at Monticello." Thomas Jefferson died as he wished on July 4, 1826—fifty years after he had written the Declaration of Independence. That very year, some claim, Ellen Wayles Randolph, a favorite granddaughter, commissioned an artist to do a watercolor of the house (*below*). On the lawn three of Mr. Jefferson's grandchildren are enjoying the Virginia spring at Monticello. The house symbolizes the man: stately, classic, enigmatic, complex—unique. "The Old Plantation" (*opposite, right*) was painted on paper in the late 18th-century by an unknown artist. It is believed to have been done on a plantation between Charleston and Orangeburg, S.C. The artist captured the spirited nature of these undefeated slaves while dancing.

OPPOSITE: From the Collection of T.J. Coolidge, Jr.
 photographed by George M. Cushing
TOP: Courtesy, Abby Aldrich Rockefeller Folk Art Collection,
 Williamsburg, Virginia
BELOW: Courtesy, Thomas Jefferson Memorial Foundation Inc.

15

North Carolina—Citadel of the Independent Spirit

NORTH AND SOUTH CAROLINA were originally one colony—named after King Charles I, who granted the area to eight lords proprietor in 1663. Though attempts were many to settle the colony, it was not until 1705 that a permanent community, Bath, was established. By 1729 the colony was so prosperous and militarily important that George II bought it from the proprietors and made it a royal colony. Shortly afterward, he split it into two colonies, North and South Carolina. The early settlers came mostly from Virginia, Maryland, and Pennsylvania. Also hundreds of free thinkers seeking religious freedom came over from Germany and Switzerland. Five years before the Declaration of Independence, North Carolinians rebelled against English rule. Later, these fiercely individualistic citizens delayed ratifying the Constitution because they felt it gave too much power to the federal government. North Carolina lacked seaports and the kinds of rivers that made for good transportation; therefore, fewer large plantations with great houses were found than in neighboring colonies. Nevertheless, there were some especially fine mansions built before the War Between the States. Two of them, Tryon Palace and the John Wright Stanly House, are shown here.

JOHN WRIGHT STANLY HOUSE, Tryon Palace Complex, New Bern, North Carolina. Completed in the 1780s, the house (*left, top* and *above*) was purchased shortly afterward by North Carolina Revolutionary leader John Wright Stanly. Architectural authority Thomas Tileston Waterman wrote: "In style it has no counterpart in the State, partaking more of the character of Hudson River mansions . . . ." The superb paneled drawing room (*left*) is replete with rare antique furniture, carpets, and objets d'art—making the place one of the South's most noteworthy exhibition houses President Washington spent two nights in the house in 1791, and in 1862 it was the headquarters of Union General Burnside. Shown here (*left, top*) is a drawing of the facade done at the time. It is from a history of the Fifth Regiment of the Rhode Island Heavy Artillery. Stanly House originally stood at Middle and New Streets. In 1966 it was moved to its present site, where authentic restoration was completed.

OPPOSITE, ABOVE: Courtesy, University of North Carolina Library
OPPOSITE, BELOW AND ABOVE: Courtesy, Tryon Palace Commission

"The Most Beautiful Building in the Colonial Americas"

TRYON PALACE, New Bern, North Carolina. From its completion in 1770 until the Revolution, this magnificent mansion (*right*) was the capitol and residence of the governor of the royal colony of North Carolina. The palace was designed in the "pure English taste" by an English architect. Contemporaries acclaimed it The Most Beautiful Building in the Colonial Americas. After the Revolution, Tryon Palace was the State Capitol until 1794, when the seat of government was moved to Raleigh. In 1798 a flash fire destroyed the main building. Over a hundred and fifty years later, during the 1950s, funds were provided for reconstruction. Fortunately, the original plans of the palace survived; these, along with numerous artifacts discovered while excavating the site, made possible the rebuilding, which was meticulously carried out. The inventory of Royal Governor William Tryon provided the necessary information for refurnishing. Paneling, mantels, doorways, furniture, and bibelots were carefully selected in England and brought over for the restored palace. The gardens (*below, left* and *right*) cover six acres and are perfect 18th-century re-creations. Myriad multicolored tulips form a tapestry of dazzling brilliance each spring.

ALL PHOTOGRAPHS: Courtesy, Tryon Palace Commission

South Carolina—Where Gardens Equal Houses in Grandeur

IN 1680, over sixty years after the founding of Jamestown in Virginia, Charleston was established—the first permanent settlement in the southern part of Carolina, which became the royal colony of South Carolina in 1729. The settlement was named for Charles II, who was then on the throne. The first settlers were proud Englishmen, clever Huguenots (French Protestants), and sturdy Dutchmen. Intermarriages soon occurred. Some believe that it was this mixing of strains that produced the reputed South Carolina spirit—dashing, tenacious, fiery. At first, the planters concentrated on tobacco; only a small amount of cotton was grown. The cultivation of rice, however, soon took the lead—it flourished in the marshy tidewater area. In the 1740s, indigo became South Carolina's second staple. The colonists felt especially close to the Mother Country until the Stamp Act in 1765. Public sentiment quickly changed after this and other British actions. In March, 1776, an independent government of South Carolina was set up with a president as its head! It is not surprising, therefore, that South Carolina was the first state to secede in 1860. And the shot that started the Civil War was fired in the Charleston harbor. Though much damage was done during the war, many of South Carolina's great plantation and town houses survived—framed by spectacular gardens resplendent with towering magnolias, huge mimosas, and massive banks of azaleas. Following are six magnificent survivors.

DRAYTON HALL, near Charleston, South Carolina. Built for Royal Council member John Drayton about 1740, this splendid Early Georgian house is a blend of Palladio and Wren (*opposite*). It stands on some 100 acres, facing the Ashley River. The land front has a magnificent two-storied pedimented portico, which is reached by a grand double stair, resting against the raised basement. The interior boasts wood paneling and ornamental ceilings of rare beauty. The great dining room is *over* the entrance hall. In the center of the overmantel (*above*) is the coat of arms of the Drayton family. Drayton Hall is unquestionably one of the finest houses in America; architectural authority Samuel Chamberlain called it "the finest untouched example of Georgian architecture still standing in America."

ABOVE: Courtesy, Collection of the Library of Congress
OPPOSITE: Courtesy, National Trust for Historic Preservation, Washington D.C.

"A Garden as Fine as Any in Europe"

MIDDLETON PLACE, near Charleston, South Carolina. Pillaged during the Revolution, burned at the close of the Civil War, toppled by earthquake in 1886, the plantation of the Middletons has in large part miraculously survived. It epitomizes the grandeur and grace of antebellum Southern country life. Renowned for its history and its breathtaking gardens, Middleton Place borders the Ashley River. It has remained in this illustrious family since its founding in the late 17th-century—serving as home and plantation headquarters during the golden ages of rice, indigo, and cotton. More than large landowners, the Middletons have, first and foremost, been public servants. Henry Middleton served as second president of the First Continental Congress. His son Arthur signed the Declaration of Independence. His grandson Henry was governor of South Carolina and America's first minister to Russia. His great-grandson Williams was a signer of the Ordinance of Secession. The Middletons are to South Carolina what the Randolphs are to Virginia. The surviving building, the south flanker (*opposite, left*), was built in 1755 as a gentlemen's guest wing. It is filled with family memorabilia. The north bedroom (*below*), for use in the summer, is graced with a "rice bed" (rice motif on footposts) festooned with mosquito netting. The geometric layout of the gardens, among the finest in the world, are seen from the air (*above*). America's oldest landscaped gardens, they were laid out by a hundred slaves, who labored for a decade. Recently, garden authority Peter Coats pronounced them "as fine as any in Europe."

ALL PHOTOGRAPHS: Courtesy, Middleton Place Foundation

OPPOSITE, ABOVE: Courtesy, Historic Charleston Foundation
OPPOSITE, BELOW: Courtesy, Carolina Art Association, Gibbes Art Gallery
ABOVE, LEFT: Photograph by Louis Schwartz
ABOVE RIGHT: Courtesy, Country Beautiful, photograph by Douglas Green
RIGHT: Courtesy, Historic Charleston Foundation, photograph by Louis Schwartz

NATHANIEL RUSSELL HOUSE, Charleston, South Carolina. One of the South's most elegant town houses (*opposite page*), it was built in 1811 by a former Rhode Island merchant who had the good sense to get one of his daughters married to Arthur Middleton, a signer of the Declaration of Independence. The remarkable unsupported elliptical staircase is lighted by a handsome Palladian triple window on the main floor and by oval windows above. Facing the garden is a half-octagon bay, containing oval rooms, one above the other—an early 19th-century innovation.

EDMONSTON-ALSTON HOUSE, Charleston, South Carolina. This impressive town house (*left*) was built c. 1828 by a Scotsman, Charles Edmonston. Ten years later it was purchased by a rice baron, Charles Alston. He remodeled the Regency house, adding the Greek Revival piazza and placing the Alston coat of arms on the front. The first two floors are operated as a museum by the Historic Charleston Foundation; the others are the town residence of the master of Middleton Place.

MULBERRY PLANTATION, near Charleston, South Carolina. Shown here (*below*) is the plantation street of one of the state's oldest plantations (1714) depicted by an unknown artist in the late 18th century. The outbuildings housed the overseer, slaves, coaches, and other necessaries.

MILFORD PLANTATION, near Pinewood, South Carolina. Built about 1850 by Governor John Laurence Manning, the house was so costly that it was called Manning's Folly by the locals. The bricks for the main walls were made on the plantation. The six great columns that support the portico rest on granite bases, which were brought from Rhode Island (*opposite, bottom*). The original furniture was imported from Europe, some from Paris and some purchased at the estate sale of the recently deceased Duke of Devonshire. The dining room (*left*) is oval and is graced by a glittering chandelier of the finest quality. The grand staircase (*below*) sweeps up in a rotunda. There is an especially graceful eighteenth-century canopy bed in one of the bedrooms (*opposite, top*). Near the end of the Civil War, Milford was the headquarters of a Union general, who ordered it burned. Fortunately, an underling delayed carrying out the command. News of the war's end came, so the house was saved—one of the best examples of Greek Revival architecture in the South.

The Glittering Dawn of Greek Revival

ALL PICTURES: Historic American Buildings Survey, photographed by Jack E. Boucher

Georgia—Colony with a High Purpose: Refuge for the Persecuted

GEORGIA WAS created by, and named for, King George II, who carved it from the southern part of South Carolina in 1733. He wanted the colony to serve as a buffer between the Spanish in Florida and his rich crop-exporting Carolinas. Care of the new colony was entrusted to the able and humane James Oglethorpe, first governor and founder of Savannah. His intent was to provide a refuge for Britons persecuted for indebtedness or for religious or political affiliations. In this idealistic early colony, rum and slavery were prohibited for over ten years. But King Cotton changed things radically. Oglethorpe's utopia, Savannah, was laid out in a fine geometric pattern, around squares, atop a bluff. It soon became the city home of rich planters and merchants, who built elegant houses, many of which still adorn its streets. Inland were the great plantations. Whether town or country, the houses of Georgia are among the finest in the South. Here are four memorable examples.

OWENS-THOMAS HOUSE (*above*), is one of Savannah's finest, and is considered the best example of English Regency style architecture in America. See pages 30-31 for a description of the house and views of the interior.

SHAKING THE RICE FROM THE STRAW AFTER THRESHING (*opposite, top*). This sensitively rendered watercolor, by the Southern artist Alice Ravenel Huger Smith, depicts threshing by hand using flails—the way in which it was done in Biblical times. After the grain was shaken from the straw, it was taken in baskets to the winnowing house, where the chaff was removed.

DAVENPORT HOUSE (*opposite*), Savannah, Georgia. The only Georgian mansion still standing in the city, it was built between 1815 and 1820 by Isaiah Davenport, a prominent architect and master builder who came from Rhode Island. Of English brick, the facade is distinguished by the famous double stairway, which ascends to the main floor. The drawing room, one of the most beautiful in Savannah, has handcarved woodwork of exceptional delicacy. A large center medallion in the ceiling provides the perfect crown for this queenly room. The Davenport House is the first restoration carried out by the Historic Savannah Foundation, which was organized by seven dedicated women in 1954 for the sole purpose, initially, of saving this remarkable house.

ABOVE: Courtesy, The Owens-Thomas House, Telfair Academy of Arts and Sciences
OPPOSITE, ABOVE: Courtesy, Collection of the Carolina Art Association
OPPOSITE, BELOW: Photograph by Hansell W. Ramsey

WARE'S FOLLY, Augusta, Georgia. Nicholas Ware's neighbors were stunned when they learned in 1818 that his town house was costing some $40,000 to build. So, it quickly became known as Ware's Folly (*below*). The horseshoe entrance steps have balusters with delicate mahogany railings, and, inside, a mahogany spiral staircase rises from the first floor to the attic. A notable feature of the facade is the Palladian motif of the doorways on all levels and even in the dormer. It was in this architecturally sophisticated setting that the Marquis de Lafayette danced the minuet at a ball given in his honor when he visited Augusta in 1825. Ware's Folly, despite its nickname, has survived and is serving an admirable purpose: It is now the Gertrude Herbert Memorial Institute of Art.

OWENS-THOMAS HOUSE, Savannah, Georgia. Acclaimed by many as the finest American house in the English Regency style, it was completed in 1819. Richard Richardson, a cotton merchant and banker from New Orleans, had the mansion built for his Savannah-born wife. Facing Oglethorpe Square, the house has floors of Georgia pine, and many of the walls are made of "tabby"—a mixture of burnt shells, ground shells, sand, and water. The house was stuccoed and is the color of Georgia clay. Inside are outstanding American antiques, most of which are pre-1830. In the entrance hall, two stairs rise and, at the second floor, become one, continuing like a bridge over the hall below (*opposite, top*)—an architectural feature with no parallel elsewhere. The house also contains an especially commodious kitchen (*opposite, bottom*) and wine cellar (*opposite, middle*).

ABOVE: Photograph by Frank Christian Studio
OPPOSITE, ABOVE: Courtesy, The Owens-Thomas House, Telfair Academy of the Arts and Sciences
OPPOSITE, CENTER AND BELOW: Photographs by Hansell W. Ramsey

THE DICKEY HOUSE, Stone Mountain Park, near Atlanta. Built in the late 1840s, by Thomas Dickey's son-in-law, Charles Milton Davis, this house (*below*) originally stood on a plantation in southwest Georgia. The State purchased it in 1961 and moved it to the park, where it presides over a number of other authentic buildings—overseer's house, slave cabins, coach house—which, collectively, re-create a typical antebellum Georgia plantation. The Dickey-Davis family entertained in the grand manner—there are three separate dining rooms. Adjoining the main one is the drawing room (*above*), where important guests were received. The house is distinguished by its graceful, double carved entrance stairs, and the look of quiet elegance its many architectural refinements give.

Tennessee—White Pillars in the Land of Plenty

IT WAS NOT until 1769 that a permanent settlement was established by Virginians in the uncharted wilds of what became Tennessee, named for a Cherokee village. A land-investment group, the Transylvania Company, purchased much of the land that now is Tennessee and Kentucky in 1775. That year, Daniel Boone was hired to blaze a trail across the mountains through the Cumberland Gap—the famous Wilderness Road. After several years of control by the state of North Carolina, then four years on its own as the independent State of Franklin, Tennessee joined the Union in 1796. During its frontier days, the homes of its settlers were rude huts, but when the fertile Tennessee Valley land began to yield its agricultural riches, Georgian-style houses started to appear. The grandest houses, however, came later, during the Greek Revival, when white-pillared mansions popped up almost magically overnight across the state. In the seventy-odd years from its settlement to the outbreak of the Civil War, Tennessee flourished with startling speed and became a major part of the cotton kingdom, complete with legends, heroes, and palatial houses. Shown here are five of these cotton castles.

CRAGFONT, near Gallatin, Tennessee. So named because it perches high on a rocky bluff above a rushing spring, this solid house curiously resembles a late-Georgian type in New England. The builder, General James Winchester, fought gallantly in the Revolution and was a civic leader in the early days of the state. Stone masons and ships' carpenters were brought seven hundred miles through the wilderness in 1798 from the general's native Maryland to build the house. The second floor of Cragfont is dominated by a ballroom, with galleries on two sides, from which the beautifully restored garden can be seen. Lafayette, Andrew Jackson, and Sam Houston were among the many who enjoyed the gracious hospitality of this plantation home (*above*).

ABOVE: Courtesy, Historic American Buildings Survey, photograph by Jack E. Boucher
OPPOSITE: Courtesy, Stone Mountain Memorial Association

BELMONT, Nashville, Tennessee. Not the usual type of plantation house, it was designed (1850) to be the setting for the social life in the prosperous city of Nashville. The grand ballroom is approached by an arcaded passage (*upper left*). A staircase (*lower left*) rises from the great hall, divides and passes over two wide doorways surmounted by brilliantly painted glass panels. The grounds of the house in its prime were a spectacle of grandeur unsurpassed and unrivalled in Middle Tennessee (*opposite, top;* c.1905). There were summer houses, marble fountains, and a brick water tower. The builder, Mrs. Adelicia Hayes Franklin Acklin, spent several seasons in France, absorbing the spirit of French architecture. A great lady, she remembered her days at Le Petit Trianon at Versailles when she planned her own little palace.

Vistas of White Colonnades

RATTLE AND SNAP, near Columbia, Tennessee. Built in 1845 by George Polk— of the family that gave the U.S. its eleventh President, James K. Polk—it is one of the finest examples of the elaborate Greek Revival house in America (*opposite, bottom*). The ten great Corinthian columns were shipped in sections from Cincinnati down the Ohio, up the Cumberland River, and then to Columbia, Tennessee. The house is still equipped with the original system of service pull bells. On the service porch are eight bells, all connected by small wires to the various rooms. Each servant knew his bell tone, and if he were a personal servant, exactly where to report.

ALL PICTURES: Courtesy Historic American Buildings Survey, photographs by Jack E. Boucher (See page 46 for a description of the ironwork at Belmont.)

Moorish Palace and Greek Temple

THE ATHENAEUM, Columbia, Tennessee. Samuel Polk Walker, nephew of President James K. Polk, built this house (*above*) in the late 1830s. Mr. Walker and his architect were obviously men of imagination—they created a miniature Moorish palace in the heart of Tennessee.

ABOVE: Courtesy, The Association for the Preservation of Tennessee Antiquities, photograph by Jesse F. Foreman
BELOW AND OPPOSITE: Courtesy, The Ladies Hermitage Association, photograph by Dan Quest Art Studio

THE HERMITAGE, near Lebanon, Tennessee. Crystal chandeliers, a winding stair, French wallpaper—all these in the home of the seventh President reveal an Andrew Jackson unknown to many. "Old Hickory" was a multileveled man. Politically, it was expedient to stress his Man-of-the-People side, and to hide his educated tastes, nicely demonstrated by the Hermitage (*opposite*). The house was built in 1835 on some 1,200 acres. A glistening white temple, it was the scene of many grand balls. Much of the inner man can be discovered by examining his library (*below*). Bookcases are filled with some 500 books, covering a wide variety of subjects. Every morning, Jackson sat in his wood-and-leather chair and opened his mail on the candlestand beside it.

The Queen of Tennessee Plantations

BELLE MEADE, Nashville, Tennessee. This is one of the South's most important showplaces. The house (*opposite, top*), built in 1853 by General William G. Harding, was inspired by the small monument of Throfyllus at the Acropolis in Athens. The architect is believed to have been the great William Strickland. The first thoroughbred horse-breeding farm in the nation was started here in 1835. It became the outstanding one in America and had an international reputation for over fifty years. Much admired are the noble proportions of Belle Meade's portico. Each of its six enormous square pillars was carved from just two stones. On entering the house, the visitor is struck by the graceful winding stair that begins in the great hall (*opposite, bottom*) and soars effortlessly to the third floor. Also striking is the drawing room, which runs the depth of the house and has two matching Adam fireplaces. On the grounds can be seen the colossal carriage house and stable. There is also a two-story brick privy (*above*), not a standard feature anywhere at the time it was built. Belle Meade's famed deer park is gone and the house is no longer the setting for endless grand parties, but all else is in splendid order.

ABOVE: Courtesy, The Collection of the Library of Congress
OPPOSITE, ABOVE AND BELOW: Courtesy, The Association for the Preservation of Tennessee Antiquities

After the War: A Southern Planter's House in Ruins

Alabama— Where Lacy Ironwork and Colonnades Abound

"ALABAMA" is a Choctaw Indian word meaning "thicket clearer." The Indians found here in the early 1500s by Spanish explorers were hard-working, successful farmers, so the name they bore suited them well. Alabama's early history is closely linked with that of its neighbor, Louisiana. The French started a community in what is now Alabama in 1702, and Mobile was founded as the capital of the Louisiana Territory in 1710. The Mobile Mardi Gras started about the same time as did the city—long before the more famous one in New Orleans. For almost a century, all settlers lived in Mobile and on plantations along the Gulf Coast. After the War of 1812 and an 1816 treaty with the Indians, this was no longer the case. Flocks of settlers from Georgia, Tennessee, Virginia, and the Carolinas rushed into the newly opened land in the northern part of the state and established large plantations, which grew cotton—more profitable than ever thanks to Eli Whitney's cotton gin. In 1819, Alabama became a state. Though there were no architects at the time, the richer planters were able to build handsome Georgian-style houses. They remembered the houses they grew up in on the Eastern Seaboard and were guided by a few architectural handbooks then available. Later, the style would change to Greek Revival, as it did across the land. Many connoisseurs, however, consider the older French and Spanish houses of Mobile to be Alabama's greatest architectural gems. Their lacy ironwork porches, balconies, and window grilles are incomparable. Following are several of Alabama's finest plantation mansions and town houses, as well as a generous sampling of the best ironwork in the area.

RIGHT: Courtesy, Historic American Buildings Survey, photograph by Jack E. Boucher

OAKLEIGH, Mobile, Alabama. James W. Roper was a successful merchant, and also something of an architect, enough so that he was able to plan the building of his home (*below*), which is now Mobile's official antebellum house. The main living quarters are on the upper floor. The double parlors (pages 42 and 43, *top*) have matching fireplaces, great sliding doors, and Oriental rugs on the heart-pine floors. The garden at Oakleigh is typical of old Mobile. There are clusters of shrubbery and the small trees popular in the 19th century. On the three and a half acres where the house stands are giant oaks and azaleas. Near the end of the Civil War, Mobile was occupied by Yankee troops, who planned to take over Oakleigh. The owner at the time was an aristocratic British woman who just happened to have an English flag in the house. Up it went on the front gallery. The Union officer arrived to be confronted by the Union Jack and the lady of the house. She must have been persuasive—no soldiers took possession of Oakleigh, and she was not disturbed again.

GAINESWOOD, Demopolis, Alabama. The grandest of all Alabama's antebellum mansions (*below*), it was built between the years 1843 and 1860 by General Nathan Bryan Whitfield, who hailed from North Carolina. Like Thomas Jefferson, Whitfield had a passion for architecture—hence the many years spent altering the size and appearance of the house. The old painting reproduced here shows Gaineswood as it looked in 1860, when it was the social center of this cotton-growing area on the Tombigbee River. Gaineswood is atypical in design; it follows no standard plan. Over the twenty-odd years that the house was built and rebuilt, styles shifted from Greek Revival to Renaissance Revival to Italianate, and Whitfield incorporated each one into Gaineswood. The result is an amazing blend not to be found elsewhere. The grounds were enhanced by balustraded terraces, statuary, and a small lake. In 1971 the state of Alabama began restoring the house for public view. The major work is finished—Gaineswood is once again Alabama's plantation palace.

LEFT AND ABOVE: Courtesy, Historic American Buildings Survey, photograph by Jack E. Boucher
BELOW: Courtesy, the Collection of the Library of Congress

Glowing Symbols of the Lost Cause

BISHOP PORTIER HOUSE, Mobile, Alabama. Shown here (*opposite, top*) is a detail of the unusual and delicate "arrow" balustrade on the main staircase of this historic old town house.

WHITE HOUSE OF THE CONFEDERACY, Montgomery, Alabama. The first home of the Confederacy was here, established on February 4, 1861. President Jefferson Davis lived in the house until May of the year, when the headquarters of the Confederate States was moved to Richmond, Virginia. Shown here (*opposite, bottom*) is the bedroom he used while in residence. Note his hatbox and valise at the foot of the bed.

BRAGG-MITCHELL HOUSE (*above*), Mobile, Alabama. Under a canopy of oaks stands this quintessential Southern mansion. It was built in 1855 by Judge John Bragg, brother of the famous Confederate General Braxton Bragg. In style, the house is a mixture of Greek Revival and Italianate motifs. Slender fluted columns ornament the three-sided verandah. Inside, there is a magnificent fifty-foot double parlor with elaborate marble mantels. The oaks on the lawn grew from acorns planted to replace trees that had been cut to facilitate shelling of the Yankee troops. The house is now owned by the Mitchell Foundation and is open to the public.

OPPOSITE, ABOVE: Courtesy, Historic American Buildings Survey, photograph by Jack E. Boucher
OPPOSITE, BELOW: Courtesy, the Collection of the Library of Congress, photograph by W.M. Manning, 1934
ABOVE: Courtesy, Mobile Historic Development Commission

Ornamental Ironwork— Indestructible Lace

THE CRAZE FOR cast iron as a decorative building material, as well as for practically everything from furniture to lamp posts, swept the country during the 1850s. It was especially the rage in the Deep South. Every possible design could be rendered in the metal, and the cost was reasonable because the molds could be used countless times. Cast iron as a facade was popular for public and commercial buildings. On private houses it was mainly used for columns and balconies. Not only was cast iron valued for its beauty but also for its practical side—it was virtually indestructible. A coat of paint now and then ensured its lasting for many lifetimes, never seriously damaged by the elements, as were wood and stone. Though most often painted a dark color, cast iron was also white, gray, and cream.

BELMONT, Nashville, Tennessee. On the spectacular grounds of this estate are five tea houses of cast iron. Shown here (*above*) is one of the smaller ones: a particularly fanciful octagonal creation topped by a pointed roof with flared projections looking like raised eyebrows. The tea houses at Belmont, as well as the balconies on the great house (see pages 34-35) are the earliest examples of cast-iron work in Middle Tennessee. Because of their highly imaginative designs, they were quickly copied elsewhere.

RICHARDS-DAR HOUSE, Mobile, Alabama. A magnificent assemblage of lacy cast iron forms the entrance porch of this historic town house (*opposite*) built in 1860 by Charles G. Richards. A native of Maine, Richards became a Mississippi steamboat captain and amassed a sizable fortune. Happily he was rich in good taste as well. The panels of the railings of his porch carry deftly executed representations of the four seasons. The interior of the house is equal in splendor to its cast-iron entrance. Open to the public, it is maintained by six local chapters of the Daughters of the American Revolution.

ABOVE: Historic American Buildings Survey, photograph by Jack E. Boucher
OPPOSITE: Courtesy, Mobile Historic Development Commission

Southern Ironwork—
The Ever-Present Decorative Accent

FOR THE Southerner, it is not enough that an object be utilitarian; it must also be pleasing to the eye. Beauty and practicality are at best combined, but in many instances beauty is the aspect most desired. The 19th-century Southerner's love of adornment found a perfect means of fulfillment in ironwork. The imagination could be given full play, and often was. Here are four splendid examples of this Southern artistic expression: A quiet little cemetery in Louisiana is entered through an iron gate (*opposite*) with a delicate leafy branch serving as an arch. A superb illustration of art imitating nature. In Mobile, Alabama, ironwork provides elegant accents on city hall (*above*). Especially fine is the graceful fanlike display of ironwork in the arch over the gate to the building. Also noteworthy is a cast-iron grave marker (*below, left*) in one of Mobile's old cemeteries. Appropriately, a moss-draped tree is depicted. Under it sit two faithful lambs on a bed of flowers. Cast iron was quite naturally ideal for fences. Shown here (*below, right*) is a section of a grand fence in Natchez, Mississippi. Exceptionally ornate in design, it proudly protects the house it surrounds.

OPPOSITE: Courtesy, Mr. and Mrs. William H. Rapp, photographers
ABOVE: Historic American Buildings Survey, photograph by Jack E. Boucher
BELOW, LEFT AND RIGHT: Courtesy, Mr. and Mrs. William H. Rapp, photographers

Mississippi—Mansions, Magnolias, and Mockingbirds

NAMED FOR its great river—The Father of Waters—Mississippi was first settled by the French near Biloxi on the Gulf Coast, in 1699. Upstate, at Natchez, a fort was built in 1716 to protect travelers going from French Canada to the Louisiana Territory by way of the Mississippi valley. The French colonists, called Creoles, established rice and tobacco plantations along the coast as early as 1719. Mississippi became a state in 1817. Soon settlers from the Easter Seaboard, and later Europe, swarmed into the area, buying as much of the rich land—perfect for growing the now-popular cotton—as possible. The pell-mell rush for great wealth was on and would, with time out for the panic of 1837, last right up to the War for Southern Independence. Northern Mississippi was the scene of some of the fiercest fighting. Some historians claim that General Grant's taking of Vicksburg sealed the fate of the Confederacy. It was after General Sherman had burned the city of Jackson that he said "War is Hell." And it was indeed hell for Mississippi: the state was left in shambles. Today, for the most part thriving, it offers remarkable glimpses into its colorful past through its many old houses, which range from the small and unostentatious (*above*) to the astonishingly large and grandiose. Both types await the visitor, and most of them are in superb condition—beautifully maintained right down to the original silver, china, books, and paintings.

ROWAN OAK, Oxford, Mississippi. Novelist William Faulkner bought this classically severe house in 1930 and made numerous alterations to the c. 1840 structure (*opposite*). The office, where he wrote, is now a literary shrine. Ancient cedars line the approach to the house, which enjoys a secluded wooded setting—the major attraction for the great Southern writer.

ABOVE: Courtesy, Special Collections Division, Tulane University Library
OPPOSITE: Historic American Buildings Survey, photograph by Jack E. Boucher

WAVERLEY, near Columbus, Mississippi. For Georgia-born George H. Young, the cupola was the thing. Octagonal and the size of a drawing room, it crowns his "big house" (*below*), which was the last word in luxury when it was built in 1855. The chandeliers burned gas, and there were several bathtubs.

ROUTHLAND, Natchez, Mississippi. Shown here (*near right*) is the long gallery of this large plantation-type house, built in 1817 by John Routh, one of the richest planters of his day. At the end of the gallery, the Confederate flag flies proudly.

ELMS COURT, Natchez, Mississippi. A handsome punka (*far right, top*) still swings over the dining-room table in the dining room. A servant at the end of the rope keeps the large fan moving.

WIGWAM, Natchez, Mississippi. This sparkling chandelier (*far right, bottom*) hangs from the music-room ceiling, painted by the Frenchman Dominique Canova. One of the oldest houses in Natchez, Wigwam was built in 1790.

LEFT: Courtesy, Historic American Buildings Survey, photograph by Jack E. Boucher.
ABOVE, LEFT: Courtesy, Pilgrimage Garden Club, Natchez, Miss.
ABOVE, RIGHT AND BELOW: Photograph by Robert Kornfeld

The Final Flowering of Plantation Life

GOVERNOR'S MANSION, Jackson, Mississippi. Built c. 1839, it is distinguished by its elegant semicircular portico (*opposite, top*). The mansion stands on a busy downtown street corner.

LONGWOOD, Natchez, Mississippi. Known as Nutt's Folly, it was begun in 1860 by Dr. Haller Nutt, a rich planter-physician. Construction was abruptly stopped by the outbreak of the Civil War. The workmen, eager to join the Confederate Army, dropped their tools, which could, until the 1960s, be seen lying dust covered and decaying about the vast unfinished rooms. Longwood is the largest octagonal house standing in America, a bizarre example of the mid-nineteenth-century Oriental style (*opposite, bottom*).

STANTON HALL, Natchez, Mississippi. One of the most famous of all Southern mansions (*above*), it is as ornate and grandiose as any house built in antebellum America. Frederick Stanton, a rich cotton broker, had it erected in 1853-58. No expense was spared—the interior doors are mahogany; the mantels, Carrara marble; the chandeliers, bronze. All European-made fixtures were brought over on a specially chartered ship: The east side of the main floor can be opened up into a ballroom, running from front to back. Immense gilt mirrors, at opposite ends, give an illusion of even greater length. Though four huge Corinthian columns dominate the facade, Stanton Hall is by no means strictly Greek Revival—the fireplaces, chandeliers, and other appointments are pure Victorian. Restored by the Pilgrimage Garden Club, it now serves as their headquarters.

OPPOSITE ABOVE: Historic American Buildings Survey, photograph by Jack E. Boucher
OPPOSITE: BELOW: William H. Rapp, Philadelphia
ABOVE: Courtesy, Pilgrimage Garden Club, Natchez, Mississippi

ABOVE: Photograph by Robert Kornfeld
OPPOSITE: Courtesy, Pilgrimage Garden Club, Natchez, Miss.

THE ELMS, Natchez, Mississippi. Amid great elm trees and sturdy live oaks, this mellow, rambling house (*below*)—surrounded by long galleries bannistered with graceful iron grilles—was built about 1782 during the Spanish era of Natchez. A striking feature of the interior is a wrought-iron stairway unlike any other in America. It is believed to have been imported from Portugal. The Elms is famous for its gardens—winding walks pass flower beds of flaming verbenas, brilliant azaleas, and old-fashioned petunias. Here and there, giant yuccas stand stiff as formal guards, with white-plumed headdress.

HAMPTON HALL, Woodville, Mississippi. Formerly known as Ararat because of its commanding position on a hill, this white-pillared mansion (*opposite*) was built in 1832 by a planter whose name has been lost. Colonel Hoard, an engineer who helped plan the Erie Canal, bought Hampton Hall in the mid-19th-century. It is famous for its spiral staircase, which soars elliptically for three stories. Live oaks almost hide the facade, and under them grow old boxwood and sweet olives. Camellias dot the lawn, adding splashes of vibrant color to the setting of this superb example of Greek Revival architecture.

Texas—Land of Cowboys and Cavaliers

THE HISTORY OF the Lone Star State is a long and turbulent one, going back to some 25 years after Columbus discovered America. Though he had not planned to, Cabeza de Vaca visited Texas in 1528, when his ship went aground near what is today the city of Galveston. Coronado also set foot on Texas soil. He brought with him a missionary who was promptly martyred by the Indians he had tried to convert. In 1821, Mexico, of which Texas was then a part, separated from Spain and set itself up as a republic. That same year, Stephen F. Austin, a Virginian, brought 300 families from the United States to Texas. The first of several "colonies," it thrived on the banks of the Brazos River. The majority of these settlers were Southerners. Before long, the inevitable happened—Revolution. The Southern colonists, unable to be Mexicans, wanted independence. The first congress of what would soon become the Texas republic met in November of 1835 in a large Louisiana-style plantation house (*above*). In 1836, independence was official—despite the temporary Mexican triumph in San Antonio at a small mission fort called the Alamo. For almost 10 years, Texas was a republic. In 1845, however, the growing desire of "Texians" (as they first called themselves) for statehood peaked, and Texas entered the Union. A land of sharp cultural contrasts—Southern, Mexican, Western—Texas was Southern enough for its citizens to cast their lot with the Confederacy in 1861. The most Southern part of the state is East Texas, where, in the mid-19th century cane, cotton, and rice began to be grown. Overnight, crude shelters were replaced by white-columned brick and frame mansions. Many of them still stand. Here are two of exceptional architectural distinction.

ABOVE: From Baker, De Witt Clinton, *Texas and Its People*, New York: 1887
OPPOSITE: Photograph by Helga Photo Studio, reproduced by permission of *The Magazine* ANTIQUES

HATFIELD PLANTATION (*below*), Washington County, Texas. One of the most imposing plantation houses of antebellum Texas, Hatfield was built around 1856 by Basil Muse Hatfield, a member of Stephen F. Austin's fifth colony of settlers. The walls of the house are over thirteen inches thick, and are of soft, sun-dried brick, made by hand from clay found on the place. Construction was undertaken with great care. The *Washington American* of July 9, 1856, carried the following: "Our attention was called the other day while taking a ride in the country to the commencement of a large brick building by Captain Hatfield at his plantation designed for a family residence. It will be a magnificent building when finished—cost probably some eight or ten thousand dollars." In style, Hatfield is akin to early 19th-century houses in Kentucky rather than to other Texas houses of the 1850s. Reared in Kentucky, Basil Hatfield obviously wanted a re-creation of his childhood home in the bluegrass.

NICHOLS-RICE-CHERRY HOUSE, Houston, Texas. Built about 1850 by Ebenezer B. Nichols, formerly of Cooperstown, New York, this neo-Greek temple stands in the shadow of skyscrapers in Sam Houston Park (*opposite*). When it was built, it was the last word in elegance—Houston, at the time, was just a boom town on the Texas frontier. The house has an unusually fine entrance door: inset columns on either side support a beautifully carved entablature. Noteworthy is the repetition of the Ionic order of columns on the second-floor level of the house—a Palladian purism few Americans of the antebellum age observed. The main stair (*above*) rises with impressive authority and is distinguished by its turkey-feather-grained wooden panels, which also appear in the columns that frame the doorways in the entrance hall. Throughout the house are superb American Empire and Gothic Revival furnishings. The second owner of this unique house was William Marsh Rice, whose vast fortune established Rice Institute. Originally, the Nichols-Rice-Cherry House stood some fifteen blocks from where it stands today. In 1959, the Harris County Heritage Society acquired the house and moved it to the park, where it was carefully rebuilt with numbered boards and planks.

ABOVE AND OPPOSITE: Courtesy, the Harris County Heritage Society, Houston, Texas

Louisiana—The Grand Parade of Plantation Splendor

DISCOVERED BY THE Spaniards about 1541, named by the French for their king, Louis XIV, in 1682—Louisiana was settled by both the Spanish and the French. Their descendants are called Creoles. Jean Baptiste Le Moyne, Sieur de Bienville, founded the capital, New Orleans, in 1718. Later, the Cajuns, French Canadians driven from Acadia (Nova Scotia) by the British in 1755, settled along the bayous near New Orleans. Then came the Americans of English, Irish, and German background. To prevent its being taken by the English, Louis XV gave Louisiana to his cousin Charles III of Spain. In 1801, Napoleon regained it for France, but no one in Louisiana was aware of this until 1803, only 20 days before the Louisiana Purchase made it a U.S. territory. This colorful history is matched by the land itself. In the northern part, hilly farms, forests, and rivers abound. In the south, things are different—live oaks draped with Spanish moss and giant cypresses with mockingbirds singing on their branches preside over fertile land crisscrossed by winding bayous. This is the delta—marvelously strange and haunting in its beauty. Agriculture started slowly in the 1750s. Indigo was the first crop, but sugar cane soon took the lead. And it was sugar as well as cotton that made princely fortunes for the planters in the mid-19th century. Early Louisiana plantation houses (*above*) were cottages raised on posts to prevent flooding. They were often surrounded by galleries onto which all rooms opened. The Greek Revival took Louisiana by storm; many of the South's most palatial houses were the result. The numerous rows of ancient oak trees provided the perfect approach for a neo-Greek temple. Here are five of Louisiana's finest architectural offerings. Two of them are the most monumental houses ever built in the South.

ABOVE: Courtesy, The Historic New Orleans Collection
OPPOSITE: Courtesy, Robert Kornfeld, photographer

OAK ALLEY, St. James's Parish, Louisiana. Some 50 miles north of New Orleans this Doric temple stands, shining in a clearing at the end of a long avenue of giant live oaks. It was built in 1836 by a rich and well-connected Creole planter, Jacques Télesphore Roman. Almost 300 years old, the oaks are 28 in number, as are the columns on the house, and the slave cabins behind. This number intrigued Monsieur Roman, who, it is said, always played his hunches. Seventy-feet square, the house is one of the finest examples of Louisiana-style Greek Revival architecture. It is topped by a white-railed belvedere, from which the fields of the plantation can be surveyed as well as the swirling Mississippi, over 300 yards away. The combination—house and alley—is one of the few that remains intact today. In most cases, either the house or the alley has disappeared— a victim of fire, neglect, or the ever-encroaching river. To view Oak Alley, shadowy-pink in color, through its tunnel of green trees is an unforgettable experience—a vision of tranquility, dignity, and pristine beauty that is forever etched in the mind.

ABOVE: Courtesy, Mr. and Mrs. William H. Rapp, photographers
OPPOSITE: Courtesy, Historic New Orleans Collection

THE PILOT'S HOUSE (*opposite*), near New Orleans, Louisiana. One of two identical pagoda-like houses, it was built by steamboat captain Paul Doullut in 1905. An architectural hybrid, the house is a unique combination of Japanese and steamboat styles. Graceful strands of cypress balls hang between the colonnettes around the gallery. The concave tile roof rises from an ornate tin cornice to a cupola, which is a version of a steamboat pilot's house. Slender tin chimneys, at either end, look like miniature columns. This whimsical house, as well as its twin, is still owned and lived in by the Doullut family.

NOTTOWAY, near Donaldsonville, Louisiana. Twenty-two columns, 50 rooms, 200 windows, 12 fireplaces, 6 stairways—all are part of this spectacular house, the second largest ever to go up in the South (*opposite, bottom,* and *below*: a 19th-century primitive painting). It was built in the late 1850s by John Hampden Randolph, a scion of one of Virginia's greatest families. He and his wife needed a large house: They had eleven children, eight of them girls. A special feature of the house is the White Ballroom—just the right showcase for displaying the eligible Randolph daughters. The ultimate in plantation splash, Nottoway is Greek Revival transformed by Italianate touches and adaptations to suit the Louisiana setting. The Randolphs managed to keep the house through the Civil War and afterward; but in 1889 Mrs. Randolph was forced to sell Nottoway. Before leaving, she made a final tour of the house, making sure that every one of the 200 windows was closed. The Randolphs had enjoyed their white castle for only 30 years.

ALL PHOTOGRAPHS: Courtesy, Mr. and Mrs. William H. Rapp

BELLE GROVE, near Donaldsonville, Louisiana. The most gargantuan house ever built in the South, it had 75 rooms, marble entrance steps, and silver doorknobs throughout. The elaborate Corinthian columns were carved from blocks of cypress 6 feet high. The brick exterior was covered by plaster painted an off-shade of pink. Architecturally, Belle Grove was a masterly potpourri of Greek Revival, Italianate, and Victorian elements. In scale it was truly monumental—the massive house rested on a 12-foot raised basement. Built by a Virginian, John Andrews, it went up shortly before the Civil War—a final expression of florid plantation exuberance.

Abandoned around 1924, this pink palace began to decay rapidly. Vandals made off with the ironwork on the galleries and the silver from the doors. And then there was the river— the Mississippi's floodwaters had been swirling closer and closer to the house for years. Like the way of life it symbolized, Belle Grove was doomed. The crumbling of walls and columns advanced, and a funereal fire brought total destruction. Shown here (*opposite, bottom,* and *below*) are views of the ruined house as it looked several years ago. Now nothing remains but charred and broken bits of stone and wood (*opposite, top*), all reminiscent of the ruins of antiquity. No one will again see the likes of Belle Grove.

Continued from page 4

founded in 1769, a long 162 years after Jamestown was first settled. One needs to be reminded that in the 1750s, when great Virginia plantations had been prospering for a century, an unhospitable wilderness stretched west all the way from the Alleghenies to the Mississippi River.

During this time up to the 1750s, however, Frenchmen far to the south had been settling on the Gulf Coast. Mobile was founded in 1702, and New Orleans in 1718, more than a century after Jamestown. French planters soon slashed out properties for themselves along the banks of the lower Mississippi, and having learned their "trade" in Santo Domingo, brought sugar cane which, they were pleased to discover, grew well in the new country.

Thus, during those years of agricultural expansion, two distinct plantation cultures emerged: the English along the Atlantic coast and the French in the deep South, both, in their respective areas, rich and aristocratic. Between them lay hundreds of miles of formidable terrain, without roads or even trails. The French, in fact, chose to link themselves, via the Mississippi River, with their fellow countrymen in Canada rather than with the English on the Atlantic seaboard.

The American Revolution and the War of 1812 finally brought the English (now American) and French Creole planters together. Since the United States had purchased the Louisiana Territory from France in 1803, all were technically fellow Americans. But the cultural chasm persisted between Yankee and Creole, until an American from Tennessee, General Andrew Jackson, won the Battle of New Orleans in the War of 1812, saving the Creoles' city from being burned to the ground by the British. From the day of Jackson's victory, the barriers between Yankee and Creole planters began to crumble.

At about the same time, three things occurred which led to a sudden splurge of wealth for America's Southern planters: Eli Whitney invented the cotton gin, speeding up the processing of raw cotton for baling and shipping; new and improved varieties of cotton were developed, producing better fibers and larger yields;

and in England, the Industrial Revolution brought new mechanical looms into use, creating thereby an insatiable demand for more and more cotton.

From 1800 to the outbreak of the Civil War in 1861, cotton was indeed king. Cotton prices were nearly always high, fertile land was cheap, and great fortunes were there to be made. The rush for waterfront property proceeded full-steam, as pioneers from Virginia and the Carolinas streamed westward across Tennessee, Kentucky, and Mississippi in search of a rich land, a rich life to go with it. French-speaking Creole planters, too, were drawn north from New Orleans, seeking a similar Eden along the bayous and rivers. Before long, almost every golden inch of Mississippi River waterfront belonged to a planter; the race for one's fortune was on.

The "cotton kingdom" boomed, and its capital was Natchez. Between 1800 and 1861, Natchez metamorphosed from an isolated provincial town to a glittering American boom town. During these rich years, one hundred great mansions rose in and near the city, and it was said that one-third of America's millionaires lived there, living like kings in huge "palaces" and adorning their ladies with silks and diamonds.

Dozens of mansions still stand in and near Natchez, many filled with treasures of the past, all silent witnesses to the city's pre-Civil War history. Today, the mansions seem cavernous and certainly impractical. After all, they were intended by the owners to be staffed by twenty-five or thirty house servants and a dozen gardeners, chosen from their hundreds, sometimes thousands, of slaves who worked on their cotton lands in Mississippi, Louisiana, and Texas.

The architectural styles of America's plantation houses derive, in part, from the architectural tastes of Queen Elizabeth I, the same lady who sent the first Englishmen across the sea to colonize America. She decided, as was her queenly prerogative, that England's medieval Gothic should be replaced by Italy's new Renaissance style. And what happened in England was naturally reflected in America, as English styles were copied in the New World as fast as their proponents could travel the ocean.

The Renaissance style, promoted by Elizabeth, was used in England for about 250 years, from the end of the old Gothic period around 1600 to the Gothic revival of 1840, embracing in time the whole American plantation period. In England, these post-Gothic styles were known as Early Stuart (1603-1649), Late Stuart (1649-1714), Early Georgian (1714-1760) and Late Georgian (1760-1820), and all were based directly or indirectly on ancient Greek or Roman models. The great architect Inigo Jones had introduced the classic, grandiose style of Andrea Palladio (1518-80) to England in the seventeenth century. Palladio had received his inspiration from the Roman ruins that abounded in his native Italy.

In America, corresponding styles were known as Jacobean, Colonial, Georgian, Federal and Greek Revival. Although it is true that after the Revolution, Americans seemed determined to split from English Georgian and create a native style of their own, most all of the

SHADOWS-ON-THE-TECH, New Iberia, Louisiana. This 1831 version of Louisiana Greek Revival (*opposite*) was built by David Weeks, in the heart of Cajun country. Despite its Georgian and Classical touches, The Shadows is basically a Creole-style house—wooden stairway on the gallery, jalousies (shutters) between the end pillars, no hallway inside. The bayou, 100 feet from the north of the house, is seen through a row of 13 ancient moss-draped oaks. Because they were planted quite close together, their branches were forced to grow upward. The Shadows is now the property of the National Trust for Historic Preservation.

From, The National Trust for Historic Preservation.

architectural designs and styles used in Southern plantation houses—and they are surprisingly diverse—were to some extent adaptations of the English originals.

And as the rich began their great era of regional building, the architecture, although attempting to reflect one way of life, never became one national homogeneous style. Mixtures of all kinds appeared, depending sometimes upon the owner's whim, sometimes upon the architect's. The basic design of a Georgian mansion might be interrupted by a wide gallery, added to provide a cool place to sit, and later on a Greek Revival portico might be added. Even new Greek Revival houses were not pure Greek; often, a gallery was added among the Parthenon-like columns at the second floor level, an insult to architectural purists but welcomed by residents on a sultry summer day. The central portion of a house in Natchez is a simple planter's cottage, but a later owner added a Greek Revival wing to one end, complete with lofty white pillars, and to the other end a red brick Georgian wing.

During the final weeks of the Civil War, a Union general was stationed in a sumptuous Greek Revival house called Milford, owned then by South Carolina Governor John L. Manning. When ordered to move on, the general told his men to burn the plantation to the ground. But before they had time to carry out his order, news came of the war's end. The house still stands today. Yet many plantation homes were destroyed during the war, or fell into ruin from neglect. And along with these great mansions went a special Southern way of life. The Civil War, the abolition of slavery, and the Reconstruction Era closed the book of the Old South. But this book, *Great Southern Mansions*, in its way can open up again a view of a unique time and a unique people, which together produced a singular architecture.

—ROBERT KORNFELD

A TRAVELER'S GUIDE

The following houses are open to the public as indicated below. For visitors' hours, it is advisable to telephone in advance.

Virginia

Carter's Grove
on US 60
6 miles southeast of Williamsburg, Virginia 23185
Open March-November. Admission charged.
(804) 229-1000

Chatham
National Military Park
Fredericksburg, Virginia 22401
Open year round. Free.
(703) 373-4461

Kenmore
1201 Washington Avenue
Fredericksburg, Virginia 22401
*Open year round, closed Monday November-October.
   Admission charged.*
(703) 373-3381

Monticello
on VA 53
3 miles southeast of Charlottesville, Virginia 22902
Open year round. Admission charged.
(703) 293-2158

Mount Vernon
on Mount Vernon Memorial Highway
9 miles south of Alexandria, Virginia 22121
(703) 780-2000

Stratford Hall
VA 3 to Lerty, 6 miles north of Montross
Stratford, Virginia 22520
Open year round. Admission charged.
(804) 493-3882

North Carolina

John Wright Stanly House
613 Pollock Street, south end of George Street
New Bern, North Carolina 28560
Open year round. Admission charged.
(919) 638-5109

Tryon Palace
613 Pollock Street, south end of George Street
New Bern, North Carolina 28560
Open year round. Admission charged.
(919) 638-5109

South Carolina

Drayton Hall
Ashley River Road, State Route 61
12 miles northwest of Charleston, South Carolina
   29407
*Open year round. Reservations only.
   Admission charged.*
(803) 766-0313

Edmonston-Alston House
21 E. Battery Street
Charleston, South Carolina 29407
Open year round. Admission charged.
(803) 722-7171

Middleton Place
on Highway 61
15 miles northwest of Charleston, South Carolina 29407
Open year round. Admission charged.
(803) 556-6020

Nathaniel Russell House
51 Meeting Road
Charleston, South Carolina 29405
Open year round. Admission charged.
(803) 723-1624

Georgia

Dickey House (Stone Mountain Park)
on US 78
16 miles northeast of Atlanta, Georgia 30304
Open year round. Admission charged.
(404) 469-9831

Owens-Thomas House
124 Abercorn Street
Savannah, Georgia 31401
Closed September. Admission charged.
(912) 234-1809

Ware's Folly
   (Gertrude Herbert Memorial Institute of Art)
506 Telfair Street
Augusta, Georgia 30901
Year round. Free.
(404) 722-5495

Tennessee

The Athenaeum
808 Athenaeum
Columbia, Tennessee 38401
*Open May-October, November-April by appointment only.
   Admission charged.*
(615) 352-8247

Belle Meade
110 Leake Avenue, at Harding Road
7 miles southwest of Nashville, Tennessee 37205
Open year round. Admission charged.
(615) 352-7350

Belmont
Belmont Boulevard
Nashville, Tennessee 37215
By appointment only.
(615) 383-7001

Cragfont
on TENN 25 in Castalian Springs
5 miles east of Gallatin, Tennessee 37066
*Open April-October, rest of year by appointment only.
   Admission charged.*
(615) 452-7070

The Hermitage
on US 70
12 miles east of Nashville, Tennessee 37202
Open year round. Admission charged.
(615) 889-2941

Alabama

Bragg-Mitchell House
Springhill Avenue
Mobile, Alabama 36607
Not open to the public, exterior viewing only
(205) 433-5119

First White House of the Confederacy
Washington Avenue and Union Street
Montgomery, Alabama 36104
Open year round. Free.
(205) 269-7569

Gaineswood
805 S. Cedar Street
Demopolis, Alabama 36732
Open year round. Admission charged.
(205) 289-4846

Oakleigh
350 Oakleigh Place at Savannah Street
Mobile, Alabama 36617
Open year round. Admission charged.
(205) 432-1281

Richards-DAR House
256 N. Joachim Street
Mobile, Alabama 36603
Open year round. Admission charged.
(205) 438-7320

Mississippi

The Elms
215 S. Pine Street
Natchez, Mississippi 39120
Open year round. Admission charged.
(601) 445-5979

Elms Court
John R. Junkin Drive
Natchez, Mississippi 39120
*Private residence, open by appointment only.
   Admission charged.*
(601) 445-9896

Governor's Mansion
Capitol Street, between N. Congress and N. West
   Streets
Jackson, Mississippi
Open during Pilgrimage (Late March-April).
(601) 948-7575

Longwood
Lower Woodville Road
Natchez, Mississippi 39120
*Open year round, tours during Pilgrimage only
 (Early March-Early April). Admission charged.*
(601) 442-5193

Routhland
92 Winchester Road
Natchez, Mississippi 39120
*Private residence, open by appointment only.
 Admission charged.*
(601) 442-0009

Rowan Oak
Old Taylor Road
1 mile south of Oxford, Mississippi 38655
Closed most holidays. Free.
(601) 234-3284

Stanton Hall
401 High Street, 2 blocks north of US 84
Natchez, Mississippi 39120
*Open year round, tours during Pilgrimage only
 (Early March-Early April). Admission charged.*
(601) 442-6282

Waverley
via US 45, MISS 50 near West Point
10 miles northwest of Columbus, Mississippi 39701
Open year round. Admission charged.
(601) 328-4491

Wigwam
307 Oak Street
Natchez, Mississippi 39120
Open year round. Admission charged.
(601) 445-8566

Texas

Nichols-Rice-Cherry House
Sam Houston Historical Park
Houston, Texas 77002
Open year round. Admission charged.
(713) 223-8367

Louisiana

Oak Alley
on Highway 18 (River Road)
2 ½ miles west of Vacherie, Louisiana 70131
Open year round. Admission charged.
(504) 369-7151

Shadows-on-the-Teche
17 E. Main Street
New Iberia, Louisiana 70560
Open year round. Admission charged.
(318) 369-6446

ACKNOWLEDGMENTS

Many people and organizations gave generously of their knowledge and time to make this book possible. The authors would especially like to thank the following:

Historical American Buildings Survey
National Park Service
Washington, D.C.
Mr. Jack E. Boucher

Abby Aldrich Rockefeller Folk Art
  Collection
Williamsburg, Virginia

The Colonial Williamsburg Foundation
Williamsburg, Virginia

National Gallery of Art
Washington, D.C.

The National Trust for Historic Preservation
Washington, D.C.
Miss Marcia Smith

Library of Congress
Washington, D.C.
Miss Mary Ison

Kenmore Association, Inc.
Fredericksburg, Virginia
Mrs. Robert F. Snyder

Thomas Jefferson Memorial Foundation
Charlottesville, Virginia
Ms. Sydney B. Swanson

Tryon Palace Restoration
New Bern, North Carolina
Mr. Donald R. Taylor

Middleton Place Foundation
Charleston, South Carolina
Alan Powell

The Association for the Preservation of
  Tennessee Antiquities
Nashville, Tennessee
Mrs. Armistead Bond

Historic New Orleans Collection
New Orleans, Louisiana
Ms. Renée Peck

Ms. Pat Phillips
New Orleans, Louisiana

Mr. and Mrs. Wm. Reve Clark
Milford Plantation, South Carolina

Historic Charleston Foundation
Charleston, South Carolina
Mrs. Henry S. Edmunds

The Carolina Art Association
Charleston, South Carolina
Ms. Cecilia Manske

The Owens-Thomas House
Savannah, Georgia
Mrs. J. Allen Tison

Pilgrimage Garden Club
Natchez, Mississippi
Miss Hattie Stacy

The Harris County Heritage Society
Houston, Texas
Mr. Peter Rippe

Mr. and Mrs. William Rapp
Philadelphia, Pennsylvania

Mr. Wendell Garrett
Ms. Allison M. Eckardt
The Magazine Antiques
New York, New York

Mobile Historic Development Commission
Mobile, Alabama
Mr. Dwight L. Young

Alabama Historical Commission
Montgomery, Alabama
Miss Cathalynn Donelson

Historic Mobile Preservation Society
Mobile, Alabama
Mrs. Cynthia Rush